Carolina's Story

Sea Turtles Get Sick Too!

By Donna Rathmell
Photos by Barbara J. Bergwerf

This book is dedicated to the many people who devote hours of time caring for
sea turtles and their nests and to those who rehabilitate sick and injured sea turtles.
The photographer donates a portion of her royalties to the SC Aquarium's Sea Turtle Hospital.

Thanks to staff at the South Carolina Aquarium and the South Carolina Department of Natural Resources
for verifying the accuracy of the information in this book.

Publisher's Cataloging-In-Publication Data

German, Donna Rathmell.
Carolina's story : sea turtles get sick too! / by Donna Rathmell ; photography by Barbara J. Bergwerf.

p : col. ill. ; cm

Summary: The photo journal of "Carolina," a critically ill loggerhead sea turtle, as she is cared for and nursed
back to health at the Sea Turtle Hospital. Just like hospitalized children, Carolina goes through a variety of emotions and
procedures during her care, recovery process, and her eventual release back to her home- the ocean.
Includes "For Creative Minds" section with turtle fun facts and math games.

ISBN-13: 978-0-9764943-0-0 (hardcover)
ISBN-13: 978-1-934359-00-6 (pbk.)

1. Sea turtles--Juvenile literature. 2. Turtles--Juvenile literature. 3. Sea turtles. 4. Turtles. I. Bergwerf, Barbara J. II. Title.

QL666.C536 R38 2005
597.92/8   2005921088

Manufactured in China, May 2016
This product conforms to CPSIA 2008
Fourth Printing

Arbordale Publishing
formerly Sylvan Dell Publishing
Mt. Pleasant, SC 29464
www.ArbordalePublishing.com

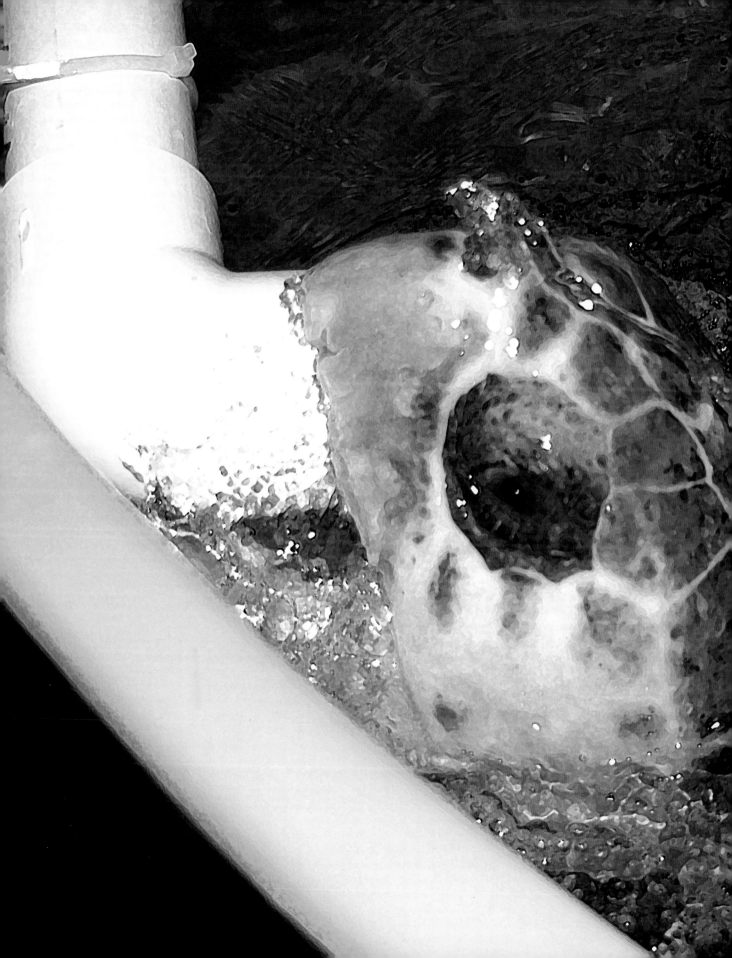

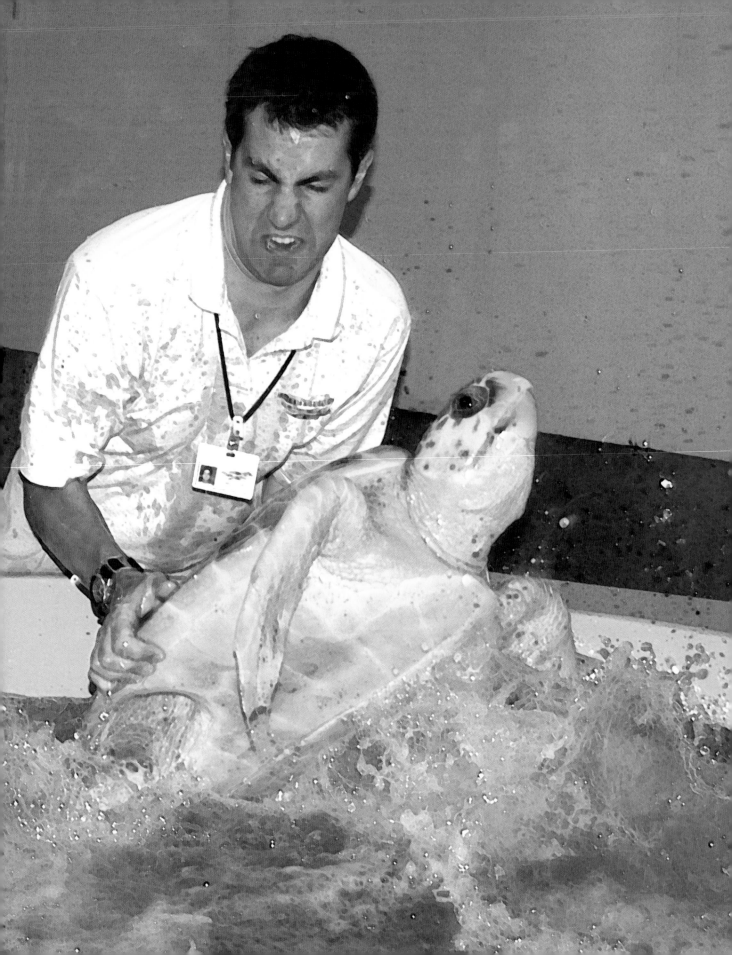

A sea turtle had been washed up on the beach. She was barely alive and really needed help from the Turtle Rescue Team.

They took her by truck to the Sea Turtle Hospital where a team of people were waiting for her.

They named the turtle Carolina.

Dr. Tom took blood samples to see what was making Carolina so sick. He looked in her mouth — "Say ahhh." She had life-threatening "turtle flu" and was lucky she was getting the help she would need.

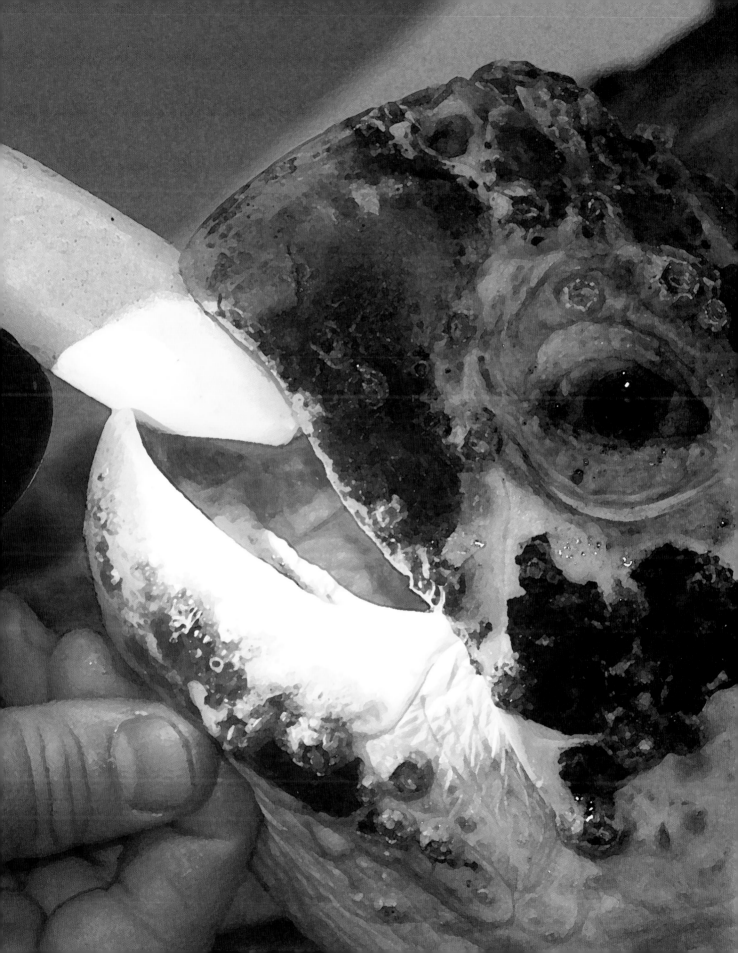

Biologist Kelly gave Carolina a shower with a hose. The shower cleaned her shell (carapace) and helped to get her blood flowing.

Carolina did not feel well and just wanted to be left alone. She even felt too sick to try to crawl away.

The next day volunteers spent hours cleaning barnacles off Carolina's shell.

Carolina did not like the feel of the brushing and scraping.

Then they rubbed antibiotic into her open sores.

Dr. Tom took some x-rays. Poor Carolina felt so sick she did not care what they were doing to her!

If she were able to cry, Carolina would have cried and cried.

Turtles get shots too! Carolina did not like getting the shots but they did help to make her feel better.

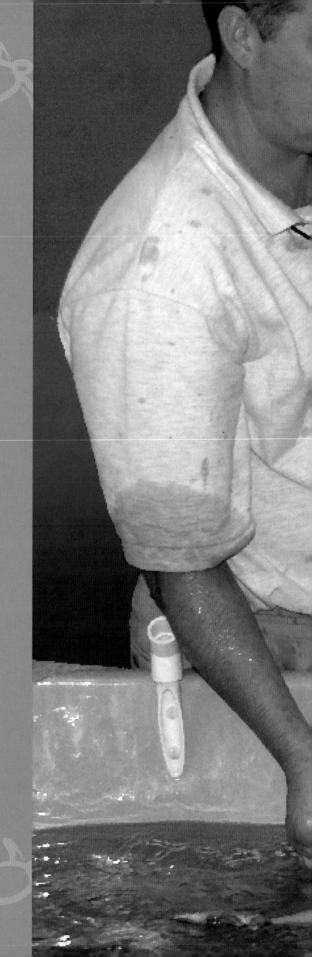

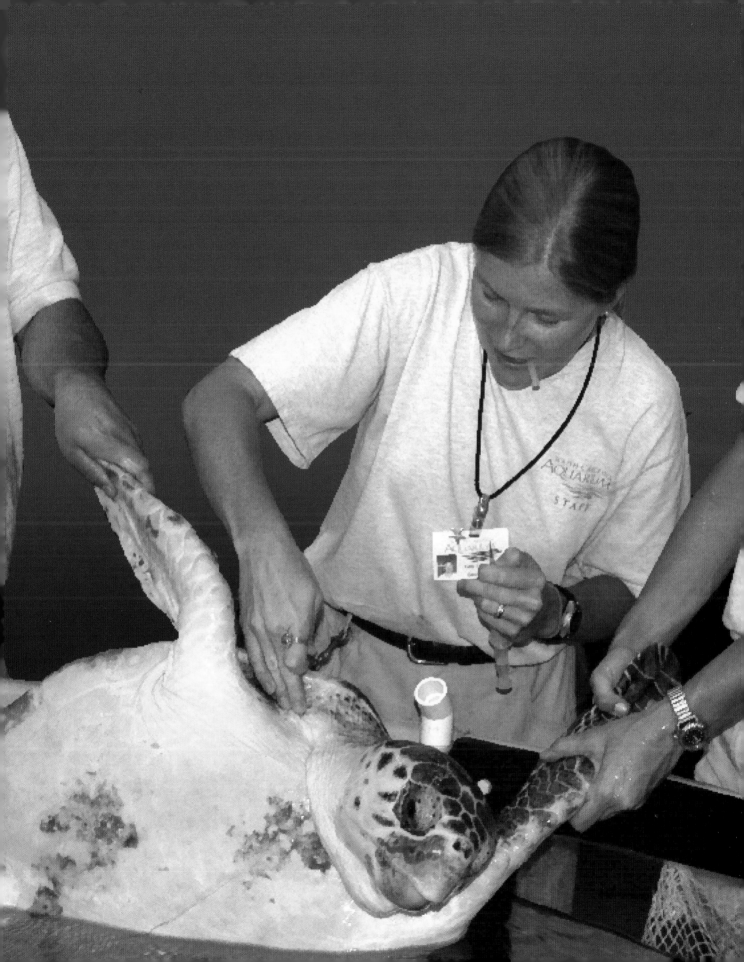

Soon Carolina was hungry. She learned that a silver-looking bowl meant food was coming. When she saw a volunteer with a bowl, she would eagerly swim over to get her dinner!

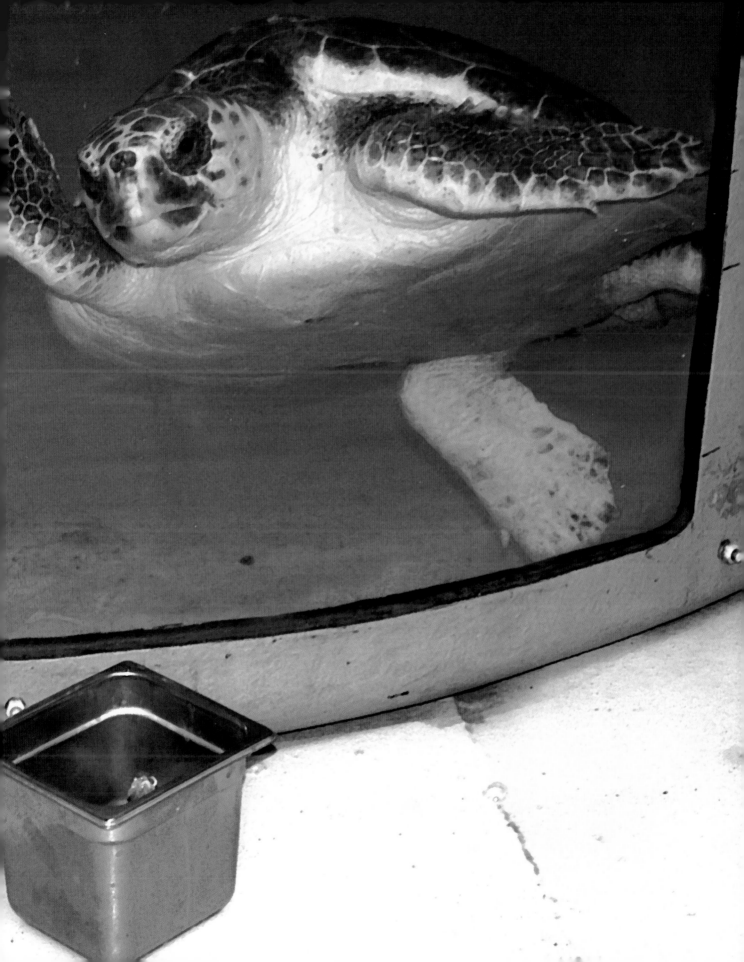

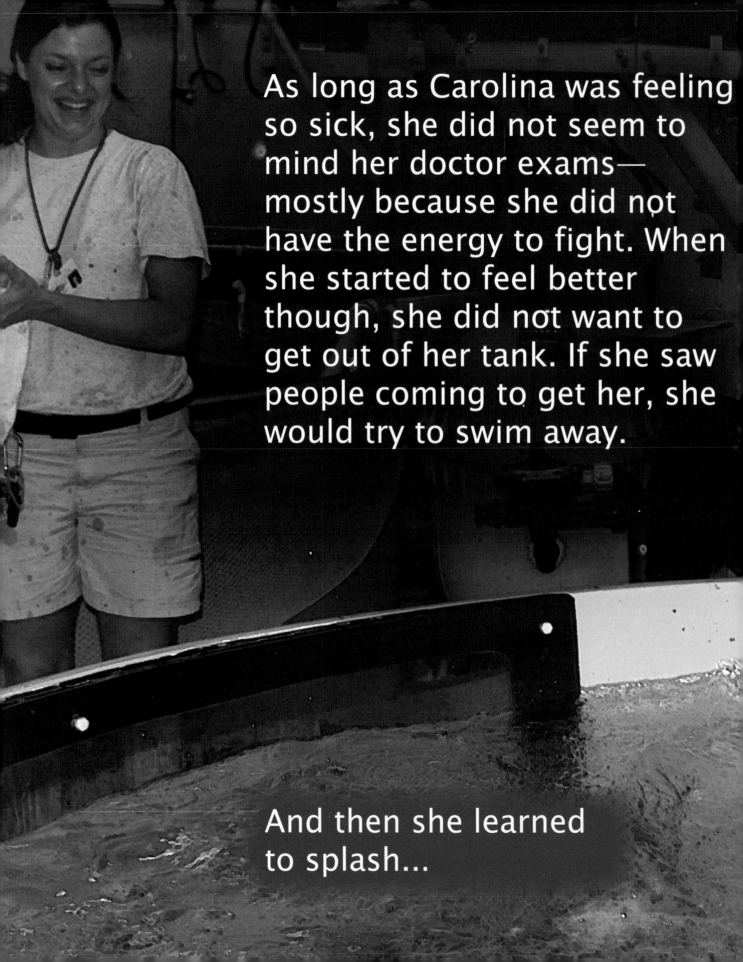

As long as Carolina was feeling so sick, she did not seem to mind her doctor exams—mostly because she did not have the energy to fight. When she started to feel better though, she did not want to get out of her tank. If she saw people coming to get her, she would try to swim away.

And then she learned to splash...

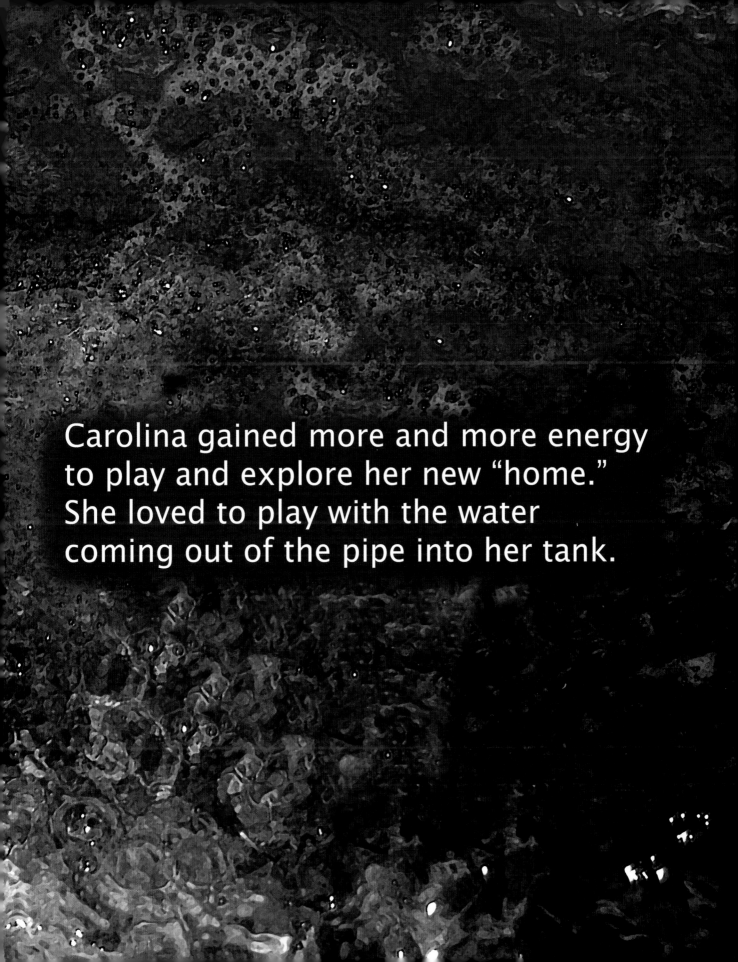

Carolina gained more and more energy
to play and explore her new "home."
She loved to play with the water
coming out of the pipe into her tank.

Carolina loved watching all the people who worked at or visited the hospital. Sometimes she would swim over to say "Hi."

She liked watching the other turtles too. It made her feel better to know she was not alone in the hospital.

Finally, the big day was here. Carolina was going home! Everyone was excited for her, but they were sad to say "good-bye" to a friend. The staff and volunteers put Carolina in a truck and took her to a beach close to where she had been found four months earlier.

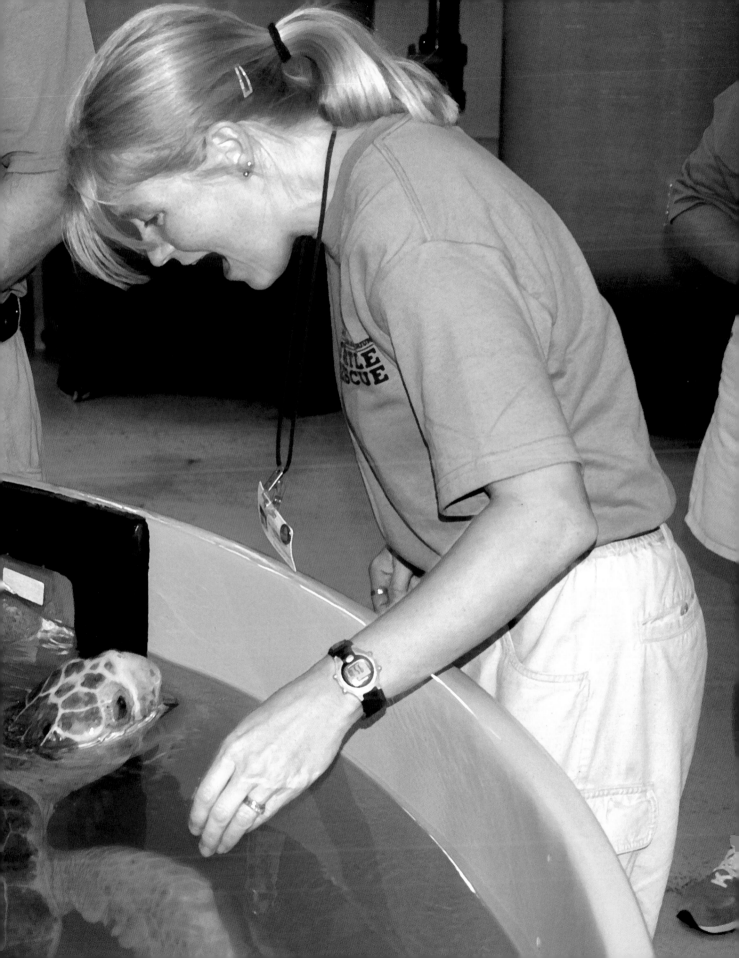

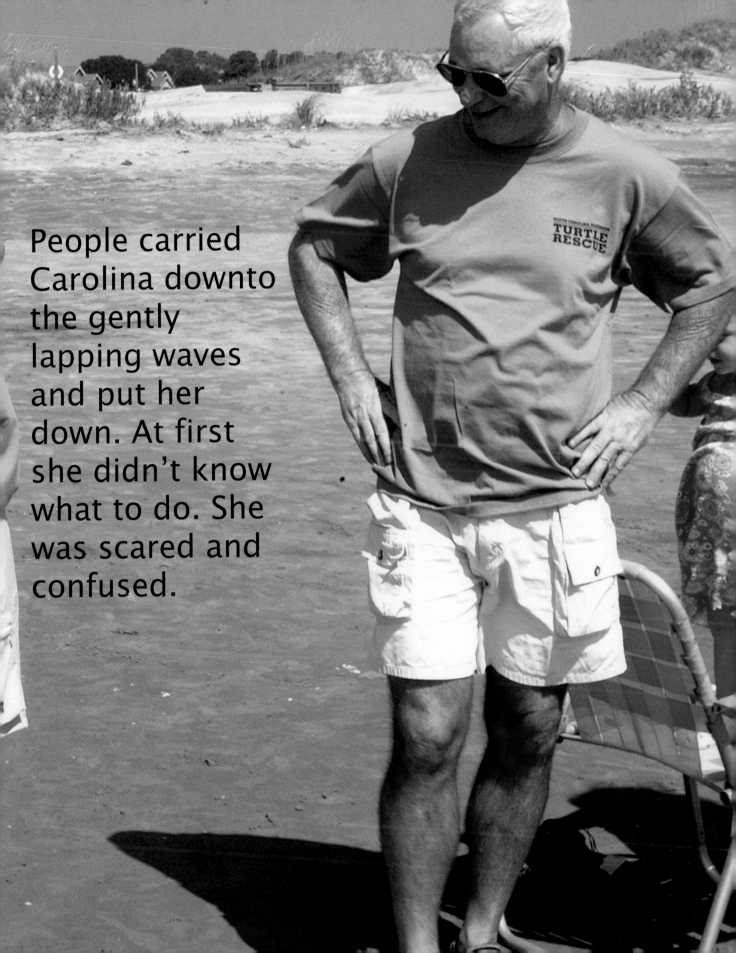

People carried Carolina downto the gently lapping waves and put her down. At first she didn't know what to do. She was scared and confused.

When Carolina felt the water wash over her, her head came up in excitement as she recognized the ocean. She hurried as fast as she could. As she felt the sand disappear from beneath her, she was thankful to all the people who had helped her when she was sick. With one final look around, she headed to the deep ocean water . . . her home.

For Creative Minds

Loggerhead Turtle Fun Facts

The top part of a turtle's shell is called a **carapace**. The bottom part is called the **plastron**. The shell is part of the turtle's body.

Sea turtles cannot pull their heads into their shells as land turtles can.

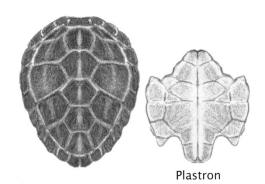

Plastron

Carapace

A female loggerhead sea turtle crawls onto the beach, digs a nest and lays 100 to 150 eggs. The eggs are about the size of ping-pong balls and hatch after about two months.

The female loggerhead hatchlings that survive into adulthood will return to the same region to lay their eggs.

For the mom and the hatchlings, one way back to the ocean is to follow the reflected light of the moon or stars.

Turtles are **reptiles**. They are **cold-blooded** and breathe air. Because they breathe air, sea turtles must come to the water's surface where they may be hit by boats.

Sea turtles, especially hatchlings, love to eat jellyfish (among other things)–because the jellyfish can't swim away. Sea turtles often mistake floating plastic bags for jellyfish. The plastic can hurt turtles and other animals. Some sea turtles can hold their breath for up to four hours while they sleep. They like to hide in rocky areas to sleep.

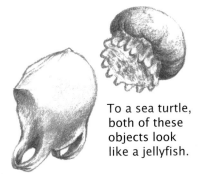

To a sea turtle, both of these objects look like a jellyfish.

A sea turtle needs sunlight to stay healthy; just like you!

How do you measure up to a loggerhead?

A full-grown loggerhead's shell is 3 to 3½ feet in diameter. A full-grown loggerhead sea turtle can weigh 360 pounds.

Make your own Sea Turtle

Directions: Do not write or color in this book. Copy, trace, or download these pages from www.ArbordalePublishing.com. Color and cut out each piece, and tape them together. The shell may be taped or glued to a paper plate for extra stability, if desired.

Sea turtles have flippers to help them swim instead of claws and/or webbed feet, like other types of land and freshwater turtles. They use their front flippers for swimming and their back flippers for steering.

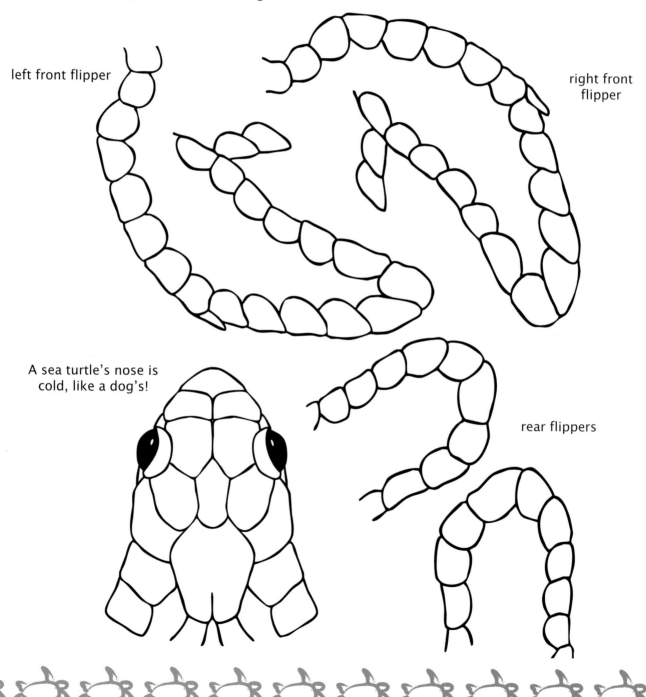

left front flipper

right front flipper

A sea turtle's nose is cold, like a dog's!

rear flippers

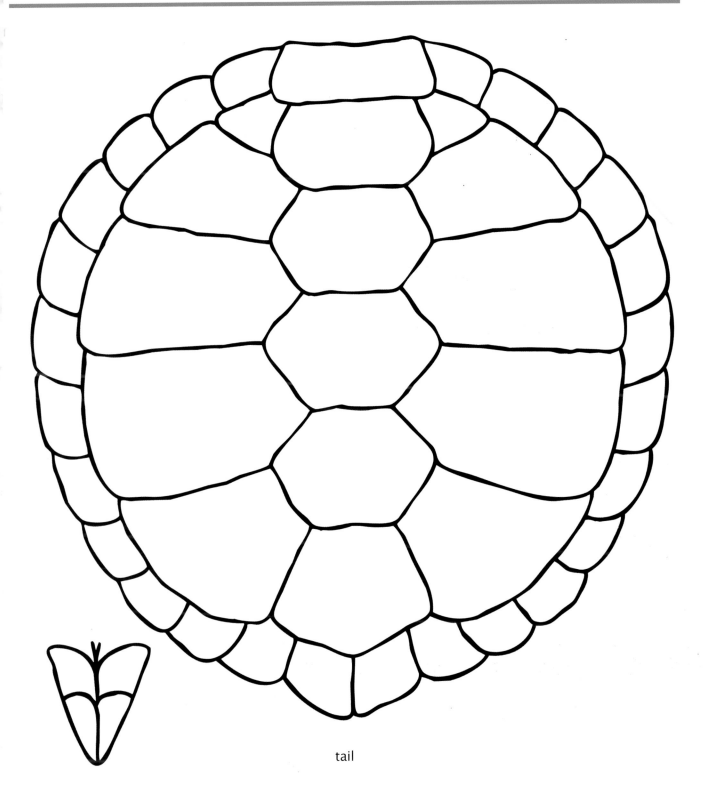

tail

Note: The sea turtle craft illustrations are not scientifically accurate for a specific sea turtle.

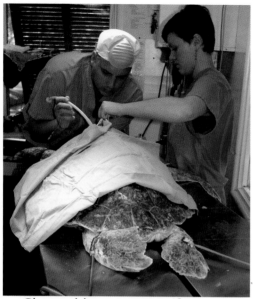

Channel has surgery after being hit by a boat.

Hamlin, who was trapped in a fishing pot line, after surgery with an IV tube. Dr. Tom tied down his flipper so he wouldn't rip the stitches.

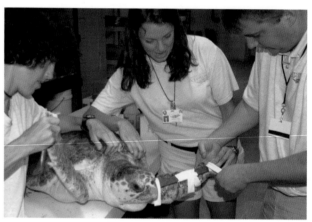

Hamlin gets a splint.

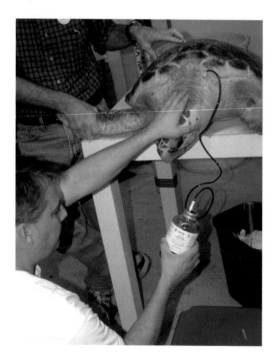

A healthy turtle donates blood for a sick turtle.

There were several other injured or sick sea turtles in the hospital with Carolina. All of the turtles seen here got better and went home to the ocean too!

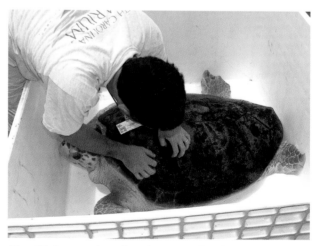

Big Girl gets her back scratched just before her release.